Cooking Delicious Meals with Air Fryer Cookbook

Quick & Easy Recipes

By

Caroline Taylor

Table of content

Asian Sticky Ribs

(Ready in about 40 minutes | Servings 4)

Per serving:

446 Calories; 29.6g Fat; 5.5g Carbs; 45.1g Protein; 4.1g Sugars

Ingredients

1 teaspoon salt

1 teaspoon cayenne pepper

1/2 teaspoon ground black pepper 2 teaspoons raw honey

2 garlic cloves, minced

1 (1-inch) piece ginger, peeled and grated 1/2 teaspoon onion powder

1/2 teaspoon porcini powder 1 teaspoon mustard seeds

1 tablespoon sweet chili sauce 1 tablespoon balsamic vinegar

1 ½ pounds pork country-style ribs

Directions

In a mixing bowl, combine the salt, cayenne pepper, black pepper, honey, garlic, ginger, onion powder, porcini powder, mustard seeds, sweet chili sauce, and balsamic vinegar.

Toss and rub the seasoning mixture all over the pork ribs.

Cook the country-style ribs at 360 degrees F for 15 minutes; flip the ribs and cook an additional 20 minutes or until they are tender inside and crisp on the outside.

Serve warm, garnished with fresh chives if desired.

Authentic Greek Pork Gyro

(Ready in about 20 minutes | Servings 2)

Per serving:

493 Calories; 26.2g Fat; 26.9g Carbs; 36.2g Protein; 7.5g Sugars

Ingredients

3/4 pound pork butt

Sea salt and ground black pepper, to taste 1/2 teaspoon red pepper flakes, crushed

1 teaspoon ground coriander 1/2 teaspoon mustard seeds 1/2 teaspoon granulated garlic 1/2 teaspoon oregano

1/2 teaspoon basil 1 teaspoon olive oil

2 pita bread, warmed 4 lettuce leaves

1 small tomato, diced

2 tablespoons red onion, chopped Tzatziki:

1/2 cup Greek-style yogurt

1 tablespoon cucumber, minced and drained

1 teaspoon fresh lemon juice 1 teaspoon fresh dill, minced

1/4 teaspoon fresh garlic, pressed

Directions

Toss the pork butt with salt, black pepper, red pepper flakes, coriander, mustard seeds, granulated garlic, oregano, basil and olive oil.

Transfer the pork butt to the Air Fryer cooking basket.

Cook the pork at 400 degrees F for 7 minutes. Turn the pork over and cook for a further 7 minutes. Shred the meat with two forks.

In the meantime, make the Tzatziki sauce by whisking all Ingredients until everything is well combined.

Spoon the pork onto each pita bread; top with Tzatziki, lettuce, tomato and red onion. Serve immediately and enjoy!

Authentic Spaghetti Bolognese

(Ready in about 30 minutes | Servings 4)

Per serving:

551 Calories; 25.9g Fat; 50.1g Carbs; 29.1g Protein; 5.5g Sugars

Ingredients

2 tablespoons olive oil

1 shallot, peeled and chopped 1 teaspoon fresh garlic, minced 1 pound lean ground pork

1 cup tomato puree

2 tablespoons apple cider vinegar 1 teaspoon oregano

1 teaspoon basil

1 teaspoon rosemary

Salt and black pepper, to taste 1 package spaghetti

1 tablespoon fresh parsley

Directions

Heat the oil in a baking pan at 380 degrees F. Then, sauté the shallots until tender about 4 minutes.

Add the garlic and ground pork; cook an additional 6 minutes, stirring and crumbling meat with a spatula.

Add the tomato puree, vinegar, and spices; cook for 4 to 6 minutes longer or until everything is heated through.

Meanwhile, bring a large pot of lightly salted water to a boil. Cook your spaghetti for 10 to 12 minutes; drain and divide between individual plates.

Top with the Bolognese sauce and serve garnished with fresh parsley. Bon appétit!

Autumn Boston Butt with Acorn Squash

(Ready in about 25 minutes + marinating time | Servings 3)

Per serving:

396 Calories; 13.3g Fat; 20.9g Carbs; 44.2g Protein; 6.3g Sugars

Ingredients

1 pound Boston butt

1 garlic clove, pressed 1/4 cup rice wine

1 teaspoon molasses

1 tablespoon Hoisin sauce

1/2 teaspoon red pepper flakes 1 teaspoon Sichuan pepper 1/2 teaspoon Himalayan salt

1/2 pound acorn squash, cut into 1/2-inch cubes

Directions

Place the Boston butt, garlic, rice wine, molasses, Hoisin sauce, red pepper flakes, Sichuan pepper and Himalayan salt in a ceramic dish.

Cover and allow it to marinate for 2 hours in your refrigerator.

Cook in the preheated Air Fryer at 400 degrees F for 10 minutes. Turn the Boston butt over and baste with the reserved marinade.

Stir the squash cubes into the cooking basket and cook for 10 minutes on the other side. Taste, adjust seasonings and serve immediately.

Bacon with Onions Rings and Remoulade Sauce

(Ready in about 15 minutes | Servings 2)

Per serving:

371 Calories; 32.7g Fat; 11.2g Carbs; 8.5g Protein; 5.3g Sugars

Ingredients

2 thick bacon slices

8 ounces onion rings, frozen 1 teaspoon yellow mustard 2 tablespoons mayonnaise 1/4 teaspoon paprika

1 teaspoon hot sauce

Salt and black pepper, to taste

Directions

Place the slices of bacon and onion rings in the Air Fryer cooking basket.

Cook the bacon and onion rings at 400 degrees F for 4 minutes; shake the basket and cook for a further 4 minutes or until cooked through.

Meanwhile, make the Remoulade sauce by whisking the remaining Ingredients. Arrange the bacon and onion rings on plates and garnish with Remoulade sauce. Bon appétit!

Balsamic Pork Chops with Asparagus

(Ready in about 15 minutes | Servings 2)

Per serving:

308 Calories; 9.4g Fat; 11.9g Carbs; 44.3g Protein; 6.6g Sugars

Ingredients

2 pork loin chops

1 pound asparagus spears, cleaned and trimmed 1 teaspoon sesame oil

2 tablespoons balsamic vinegar 1 teaspoon yellow mustard

1/2 teaspoon garlic, minced

1/2 teaspoon smoked pepper 1/4 teaspoon dried dill

Salt and black pepper, to taste

Directions

Toss the pork loin chops and asparagus with the other Ingredients until well coated on all sides.

Place the pork in the Air Fryer cooking basket and cook at 400 degrees F for 7 minutes; turn them over, top with the asparagus and continue to cook for a further 5 minutes.

Serve warm with mayo, sriracha sauce, or sour cream if desired. Bon appétit!

Blade Steaks with Butter-Fried Broccoli

(Ready in about 30 minutes | Servings 4)

Per serving:

443 Calories; 29.5g Fat; 11.3g Carbs; 34.2g Protein; 2.8g Sugars

Ingredients

1 ½ pounds blade steaks skinless, boneless Kosher salt and ground black pepper, to taste 2 garlic cloves, crushed

2 tablespoons soy sauce 1 tablespoon oyster sauce 2 tablespoon lemon juice

1 pound broccoli, broken into florets 2 tablespoons butter, melted

1 teaspoon dried dill weed

2 tablespoons sunflower seeds, lightly toasted

Directions

Start by preheating your Air Fryer to 385 degrees F. Spritz the bottom and sides of the cooking basket with cooking spray.

Now, season the pork with salt and black pepper. Add the garlic, soy sauce oyster sauce, and lemon juice.

Cook for 20 minutes; turning over halfway through the cooking time.

Toss the broccoli with the melted butter and dill. Add the broccoli to the cooking basket and cook at 400 degrees F for 6 minutes, shaking the basket periodically.

Serve the warm pork with broccoli and garnish with sunflower seeds. Bon appétit!

Boston Butt with Salsa Verde

(Ready in about 35 minutes | Servings 4)

Per serving:

374 Calories; 24.1g Fat; 8.6g Carbs; 29.9g Protein; 4.7g Sugars

Ingredients

1 pound Boston butt, thinly sliced across the grain into 2-inch-long strips
1/2 teaspoon red pepper flakes, crushed

Sea salt and ground black pepper, to taste

1/2 pound tomatillos, chopped 1 small-sized onion, chopped 2 chili peppers, chopped

2 cloves garlic

2 tablespoons fresh cilantro, chopped 1 tablespoon olive oil

1 teaspoon sea salt

Directions

Rub the Boston butt with red pepper, salt, and black pepper. Spritz the bottom of the cooking basket with a nonstick cooking spray.

Roast the Boston butt in the preheated Air Fryer at 390 degrees F for 10 minutes. Shake the basket and cook another 10 minutes.

While the pork is roasting, make the salsa.

Blend the remaining Ingredients until smooth and uniform. Transfer the mixture to a saucepan and add 1 cup of water.

Bring to a boil; reduce the heat and simmer for 8 to 12 minutes. Serve the roasted pork with the salsa verde on the side. Enjoy!

Caprese Pork Chops

(Ready in about 15 minutes + marinating time | Servings 3)

Per serving:

345 Calories; 12.9g Fat; 14.7g Carbs; 40.3g Protein; 10.8g Sugars

Ingredients

1 pound center-cut pork chops, boneless 1/4 cup balsamic vinegar

1 tablespoon honey

1 tablespoon whole-grain mustard 1/2 teaspoon olive oil

1/2 teaspoon smoked paprika

Salt and black pepper, to taste 1/2 teaspoon shallot powder 1/2 teaspoon porcini powder 1/2 teaspoon granulated garlic 3 slices fresh mozzarella

3 thick slices tomatoes

2 tablespoons fresh basil leaves, chopped

Directions

Place the pork chops, balsamic vinegar, honey, mustard, olive oil and spices in a bowl. Cover and let it marinate in your refrigerator for 1 hour.

Cook in the preheated Air Fryer at 400 degrees F for 7 minutes. Top with cheese and continue to cook for 5 minutes more.

Top with sliced tomato and basil and serve immediately.

Cheesy Creamy Pork Casserole

(Ready in about 25 minutes | Servings 4)

Per serving:

433 Calories; 20.4g Fat; 2.6g Carbs; 56.5g Protein; 0.3g Sugars

Ingredients

2 tablespoons olive oil

2 pounds pork tenderloin, cut into serving-size pieces 1 teaspoon coarse sea salt

1/2 teaspoon freshly ground pepper 1/4 teaspoon chili powder

1 teaspoon dried marjoram

1 tablespoon mustard 1 cup Ricotta cheese

1 ½ cups chicken broth

Directions

Start by preheating your Air Fryer to 350 degrees F.

Heat the olive oil in a pan over medium-high heat. Once hot, cook the pork for 6 to 7 minutes, flipping it to ensure even cooking.

Arrange the pork in a lightly greased casserole dish. Season with salt, black pepper, chili powder, and marjoram.

In a mixing dish, thoroughly combine the mustard, cheese, and chicken broth. Pour the mixture over the pork chops in the casserole dish.

Bake for another 15 minutes or until bubbly and heated through. Bon appétit!

Chinese Char Siu Pork

(Ready in about 25 minutes + marinating time | Servings 3)

Per serving:

246 Calories; 10.3g Fat; 7.8g Carbs; 28.6g Protein; 6.7g Sugars

Ingredients

1 pound pork shoulder, cut into long strips 1/2 teaspoon Chinese five-spice powder 1/4 teaspoon Szechuan pepper

1 tablespoon hoisin sauce 2 tablespoons hot water

1 teaspoon sesame oil

1 tablespoon Shaoxing wine 1 tablespoon molasses

Directions

Place all Ingredients in a ceramic dish and let it marinate for 2 hours in the refrigerator.

Cook in the preheated Air Fryer at 390 degrees F for 20 minutes, shaking the basket halfway through the cooking time.

Heat the reserved marinade in a wok for about 15 minutes or until the sauce has thickened. Spoon the sauce over the warm pork shoulder and serve with rice if desired. Enjoy!

Easy Pork & Parmesan Meatballs

(Ready in about 15 minutes | Servings 3)

Per serving:

539 Calories; 38.4g Fat; 17.5g Carbs; 29.2g Protein; 4.3g Sugars

Ingredients

1 pound ground pork

2 tablespoons tamari sauce 1 teaspoon garlic, minced

2 tablespoons spring onions, finely chopped 1 tablespoon brown sugar

1 tablespoon olive oil

1/2 cup breadcrumbs

2 tablespoons parmesan cheese, preferably freshly grated

Directions

Combine the ground pork, tamari sauce, garlic, onions, and sugar in a mixing dish. Mix until everything is well incorporated.

Form the mixture into small meatballs.

In a shallow bowl, mix the olive oil, breadcrumbs, and parmesan. Roll the meatballs over the parmesan mixture.

Cook at 380 degrees F for 3 minutes; shake the basket and cook an additional 4 minutes or until meatballs are browned on all sides. Bon appétit!

Easy Pork Pot Stickers

(Ready in about 10 minutes | Servings 2)

Per serving:

352 Calories; 13.5g Fat; 27.8g Carbs; 31.2g Protein; 2.2g Sugars

Ingredients

1/2 pound lean ground pork

1/2 teaspoon fresh ginger, freshly grated 1 teaspoon chili garlic sauce

1 tablespoon soy sauce 1 tablespoon rice wine

1/4 teaspoon Szechuan pepper

2 stalks scallions, chopped 1 tablespoon sesame oil

8 (3-inch) round wonton wrappers

Directions

Cook the ground pork in a preheated skillet until no longer pink, crumbling with a fork. Stir in the other Ingredients, except for the wonton wrappers; stir to combine well.

Place the wonton wrappers on a clean work surface. Divide the pork filling between the wrappers. Wet the edge of each wrapper with water, fold the top half over the bottom half and pinch the border to seal.

Place the pot stickers in the cooking basket and brush them with a little bit of olive oil. Cook the pot sticker at 400 degrees F for 8 minutes. Serve immediately.

Easy Pork Sandwiches

(Ready in about 55 minutes | Servings 3)

Per serving:

453 Calories; 8.9g Fat; 33.4g Carbs; 56.8g Protein; 11.6g Sugars

Ingredients

2 teaspoons peanut oil 1 ½ pounds pork sirloin

Coarse sea salt and ground black pepper, to taste

1 tablespoon smoked paprika 1/4 cup prepared barbecue sauce 3 hamburger buns, split

Directions

Start by preheating your Air Fryer to 360 degrees F.

Drizzle the oil all over the pork sirloin. Sprinkle with salt, black pepper, and paprika.

Cook for 50 minutes in the preheated Air Fryer.

Remove the roast from the Air Fryer and shred with two forks. Mix in the barbecue sauce. Serve over hamburger buns. Enjoy!

Egg Noodles with Sausage-Pepper Sauce

(Ready in about 30 minutes | Servings 4)

Per serving:

389 Calories; 32.2g Fat; 11.4g Carbs; 13.6g Protein; 5.7g Sugars

Ingredients

1 tablespoon lard, at room temperature 2 garlic cloves, smashed

2 scallions, chopped

1 red bell pepper, chopped

1 green bell pepper, chopped 1 pound pork sausages, sliced 2 ripe tomatoes, pureed

2 tablespoons tomato ketchup 1 teaspoon molasses

1 tablespoon flax seed meal Salt and black pepper, to taste 1 teaspoon basi

1 teaspoon rosemary

1 teaspoon oregano

1 package egg noodles

Directions

Melt the lard in a baking pan at 380 degrees F. Once hot, sauté the garlic, scallions, and peppers until tender about 2 minutes.

Add the sausages and cook an additional 5 minutes, stirring occasionally.

Add the tomato puree, tomato ketchup, molasses, flax seed meal, and spices; cook for 4 to 5 minutes more or until everything is thoroughly warmed and the sauce has thickened.

Meanwhile, bring a large pot of lightly salted water to a boil. Cook the egg noodles for 10 to 12 minutes; drain and divide between individual plates. Top with the warm sauce and serve. Bon appétit!

Ground Pork and Cheese Casserole

(Ready in about 45 minutes | Servings 4)

Per serving:

561 Calories; 28g Fat; 22.2g Carbs; 52.5g Protein; 7.7g Sugars

Ingredients

1 tablespoon olive oil

1 ½ pounds pork, ground

Sea salt and ground black pepper, to taste 1 medium-sized leek, sliced

1 teaspoon fresh garlic, minced 2 carrots, trimmed and sliced

1 (2-ounce) jar pimiento, drained and chopped

1 can (10 ¾-ounces) condensed cream of mushroom soup 1 cup water

1/2 cup ale

1 cup cream cheese

1/2 cup soft fresh breadcrumbs

1 tablespoon fresh cilantro, chopped

Directions

Start by preheating your Air Fryer to 320 degrees F.

Add the olive oil to a baking dish and heat for 1 to 2 minutes. Add the por salt, pepper and cook for 6 minutes, crumbling with a fork.

Add the leeks and cook for 4 to 5 minutes, stirring occasionally.

Add the garlic, carrots, pimiento, mushroom soup, water, ale, and cream cheese. Gently stir to combine.

Turn the temperature to 370 degrees F.

Top with the breadcrumbs. Place the baking dish in the cooking basket and cook approximately 30 minutes or until everything is thoroughly cooked.

Serve garnished with fresh cilantro. Bon appétit!

Herb-Crusted Pork Roast

(Ready in about 1 hour | Servings 2)

Per serving:

220 Calories; 11.4g Fat; 3.3g Carbs; 24.9g Protein; 1.7g Sugars

Ingredients

1/2 pound pork loin

Salt and black pepper, to taste 1/2 teaspoon onion powder 1/2 teaspoon parsley flakes 1/2 teaspoon oregano

1/2 teaspoon thyme

1/2 teaspoon grated lemon peel 1 teaspoon garlic, minced

1 teaspoon butter, softened

Directions

Pat the pork loin dry with kitchen towels. Season it with salt and black pepper.

In a bowl, mix the remaining Ingredients until well combined. Coat the pork with the herb rub, pressing to adhere well.

Cook in the preheated Air Fryer at 360 degrees F for 30 minutes; turn it over and cook on the other side for 25 minutes more. Bon appétit!

Herbed Pork Loin with Carrot Chips

(Ready in about 1 hour 15 minutes | Servings 4)

Per serving:

461 Calories; 25.8g Fat; 10.8g Carbs; 44g Protein; 5.3g Sugars

Ingredients

1 tablespoon peanut oil

1 ½ pounds pork loin, cut into 4 pieces

Coarse sea salt and ground black pepper, to taste 1/2 teaspoon onion powder

1 teaspoon garlic powder 1/2 teaspoon cayenne pepper 1/2 teaspoon dried rosemary 1/2 teaspoon dried basil

1/2 teaspoon dried oregano

1 pound carrots, cut into matchsticks 1 tablespoon coconut oil, melted

Directions

Drizzle 1 tablespoon of peanut oil all over the pork loin. Season with salt, black pepper, onion powder, garlic powder, cayenne pepper, rosemary, basil, and oregano.

Cook in the preheated Air Fryer at 360 degrees F for 55 minutes; make sur to turn the pork over every 15 minutes to ensure even cooking.

Test for doneness with a meat thermometer.

Toss the carrots with melted coconut oil; season to taste and cook in the preheated Air Fryer at 380 degrees F for 15 minutes.

Serve the warm pork loin with the carrots on the side. Enjoy!

Italian Nonna's Polpette

(Ready in about 15 minutes | Servings 3)

Per serving:

356 Calories; 14.4g Fat; 19.6g Carbs; 36.3g Protein; 6.8g Sugars

Ingredients

1 teaspoon olive oil

2 tablespoons green onions, chopped 1/2 teaspoon garlic, pressed

1/2 pound sweet Italian pork sausage, crumbled 1 tablespoon parsley, chopped

1/2 teaspoon cayenne pepper

Sea salt and ground black pepper, to taste 1 egg

2 tablespoons milk

1 crustless bread slice

Directions

Mix the olive oil, green onions, garlic, sausage, parsley, cayenne pepper, salt and black pepper in a bowl.

Whisk the egg and milk until pale and frothy. Soak the bread in the milk mixture. Add the soaked bread to the sausage mixture. Mix again to combine well.

Shape the mixture into 8 meatballs.

Add the meatballs to the cooking basket and cook them at 360 degrees for 5 minutes. Then, turn them and cook the other side for 5 minutes more. You can serve these meatballs over spaghetti. Bon appétit!

Italian-Style Honey Roasted Pork

(Ready in about 50 minutes | Servings 3)

Per serving:

314 Calories; 9.8g Fat; 13g Carbs; 41.8g Protein; 11.8g Sugars

Ingredients

1 teaspoon Celtic sea salt

1/2 teaspoon black pepper, freshly cracked 1/4 cup red wine

2 tablespoons mustard

2 tablespoons honey

2 garlic cloves, minced 1 pound pork top loin

1 tablespoon Italian herb seasoning blend

Directions

In a ceramic bowl, mix the salt, black pepper, red wine, mustard, honey, and garlic. Add the pork top loin and let it marinate at least 30 minutes.

Spritz the sides and bottom of the cooking basket with a nonstick cooking spray.

Place the pork top loin in the basket; sprinkle with the Italian herb seasoning blend.

Cook the pork tenderloin at 370 degrees F for 10 minutes. Flip halfway through, spraying with cooking oil and cook for 5 to 6 minutes more. Serve immediately.

Keto Crispy Pork Chops

(Ready in about 20 minutes | Servings 3)

Per serving:

467 Calories; 26.8g Fat; 2.7g Carbs; 50.3g Protein; 1.3g Sugars

Ingredients

3 center-cut pork chops, boneless 1/2 teaspoon paprika

Sea salt and ground black pepper, to taste

1/4 cup Romano cheese, grated 1/4 cup crushed pork rinds

1/2 teaspoon garlic powder

1/2 teaspoon mustard seeds 1/2 teaspoon dried marjoram 1 egg, beaten

1 tablespoon buttermilk 1 teaspoon peanut oil

Directions

Pat the pork chops dry with kitchen towels. Season them with paprika, salt and black pepper.

Add the Romano cheese, crushed pork rinds, garlic powder, mustard seeds and marjoram to a rimmed plate.

Beat the egg and buttermilk in another plate. Now, dip the pork chops in the egg, then in the cheese/pork rind mixture.

Drizzle the pork with peanut oil. Cook in the preheated Air Fryer at 400 degrees F for 12 minutes, flipping pork chops halfway through the cooking time.

Serve with keto-friendly sides such as cauliflower rice. Bon appétit!

Mexican-Style Ground Pork with Peppers

(Ready in about 40 minutes | Servings 4)

Per serving:

505 Calories; 39.4g Fat; 9.9g Carbs; 28g Protein; 5.1g Sugars

Ingredients

2 chili peppers

1 red bell pepper

2 tablespoons olive oil

1 large-sized shallot, chopped 1 pound ground pork

2 garlic cloves, minced

2 ripe tomatoes, pureed

1 teaspoon dried marjoram 1/2 teaspoon mustard seeds 1/2 teaspoon celery seeds

1 teaspoon Mexican oregano 1 tablespoon fish sauce

2 tablespoons fresh coriander, chopped Salt and ground black pepper, to taste 2 cups water

1 tablespoon chicken bouillon granules

2 tablespoons sherry wine

1 cup Mexican cheese blend

Directions

Roast the peppers in the preheated Air Fryer at 395 degrees F for 10 minutes, flipping them halfway through cook time.

Let them steam for 10 minutes; then, peel the skin and discard the stems and seeds. Slice the peppers into halves.

Heat the olive oil in a baking pan at 380 degrees F for 2 minutes; add the shallots and cook for 4 minutes. Add the ground pork and garlic; cook for a further 4 to 5 minutes.

After that, stir in the tomatoes, marjoram, mustard seeds, celery seeds, oregano, fish sauce, coriander, salt, and pepper. Add a layer of sliced peppers to the baking pan.

Mix the water with the chicken bouillon granules and sherry wine. Add the mixture to the baking pan.

Cook in the preheated Air Fryer at 395 degrees F for 10 minutes. Top with cheese and bake an additional 5 minutes until the cheese has melted. Serve immediately.

Perfect Meatball Hoagies

(Ready in about 15 minutes | Servings 2)

Per serving:

433 Calories; 16.4g Fat; 33g Carbs; 39.7g Protein; 7g Sugars

Ingredients

1/2 pound lean ground pork

1 teaspoon fresh garlic, minced

2 tablespoons fresh scallions, chopped 1 teaspoon dried basil

1/2 teaspoon dried oregano

1/2 teaspoon dried parsley flakes

Sea salt and ground black pepper, to taste 1 tablespoon soy sauce

1 egg, beaten

1/4 cup Pecorino Romano cheese, grated 1/2 cup quick-cooking oats

2 hoagie rolls

1 medium-sized tomato, sliced 2 pickled cherry peppers

Directions

In a mixing bowl, thoroughly combine the ground pork, garlic, scallions, basil, oregano, parsley, salt, black pepper, soy sauce, eggs, cheese and quick-cooking oats. Mix until well incorporated. Shape the mixture into 6 meatballs.

Add the meatballs to the cooking basket and cook them at 360 degrees for 10 minutes. Turn the meatballs halfway through the cooking time.

Cut the hoagie rolls lengthwise almost entirely through. Layer the meatballs onto the bottom of the roll.

Top with the tomato and peppers. Close the rolls, cut in half and serve immediately. Bon appétit!

Perfect Sloppy Joes

(Ready in about 30 minutes | Servings 4)

Per serving:

545 Calories; 32g Fat; 38.1g Carbs; 26.1g Protein; 3.9g Sugars

Ingredients

1 tablespoon olive oil 1 shallot, chopped

2 garlic cloves, minced

1 bell pepper, chopped 1 pound ground pork

2 ripe medium-sized tomatoes, pureed

1 tablespoon Worcestershire sauce

1 tablespoon poultry seasoning blend Dash ground allspice

6 hamburger buns

Directions

Start by preheating your Air Fryer to 390 degrees F. Heat the olive oil for a few minutes.

Once hot, sauté the shallots until just tender. Add the garlic and bell pepper; cook for 4 minutes more or until they are aromatic.

Add the ground pork and cook for 5 minutes more, crumbling with a fork. Next step, stir in the pureed tomatoes, Worcestershire sauce, and spices.

Decrease the temperature to 365 degrees F and cook another 10 minutes.

Spoon the meat mixture into hamburger buns and transfer them to the cooking basket. Cook for 7 minutes or until thoroughly warmed.

Pork Belly with New Potatoes

(Ready in about 50 minutes | Servings 4)

Per serving:

547 Calories; 30.2g Fat; 20.9g Carbs; 45.1g Protein; 1.1g Sugars

Ingredients

1 ½ pounds pork belly, cut into 4 pieces Kosher salt and ground black pepper, to taste 1 teaspoon smoked paprika

1/2 teaspoon turmeric powder 2 tablespoons oyster sauce

2 tablespoons green onions

4 cloves garlic, sliced

1 pound new potatoes, scrubbed

Directions

Preheat your Air Fryer to 390 degrees F. Pat dry the pork belly and season with all spices listed above.

Add the oyster sauce and spritz with a nonstick cooking spray on all sides. Now, cook in the preheated Air Fryer for 30 minutes. Turn them over every 10 minutes.

Increase the temperature to 400 degrees F. Add the green onions, garlic, and new potatoes.

Cook another 15 minutes, shaking occasionally. Serve warm.

Pork Cutlets with a Twist

(Ready in about 1 hour 20 minutes | Servings 2)

Per serving:

579 Calories; 19.4g Fat; 50g Carbs; 49.6g Protein; 2.2g Sugars

Ingredients

1 cup water

1 cup red wine

1 tablespoon sea salt 2 pork cutlets

1/2 cup all-purpose flour 1 teaspoon shallot powder

1/2 teaspoon porcini powder

Sea salt and ground black pepper, to taste 1 egg

1/4 cup yogurt

1 teaspoon brown mustard 1 cup tortilla chips, crushed

Directions

In a large ceramic dish, combine the water, wine and salt. Add the pork cutlets and put for 1 hour in the refrigerator.

In a shallow bowl, mix the flour, shallot powder, porcini powder, salt, and ground pepper. In another bowl, whisk the eggs with yogurt and mustard.

In a third bowl, place the crushed tortilla chips.

Dip the pork cutlets in the flour mixture and toss evenly; then, in the egg mixture. Finally, roll them over the crushed tortilla chips.

Spritz the bottom of the cooking basket with cooking oil. Add the breaded pork cutlets and cook at 395 degrees F and for 10 minutes.

Flip and cook for 5 minutes more on the other side. Serve warm.

Pork Koftas with Yoghurt Sauce

(Ready in about 25 minutes | Servings 4)

Per serving:

407 Calories; 28.5g Fat; 3.4g Carbs; 32.9g Protein; 1.3g Sugars

Ingredients

2 teaspoons olive oil 1/2 pound ground pork 1/2 pound ground beef 1 egg, whisked

Sea salt and ground black pepper, to taste 1 teaspoon paprika

2 garlic cloves, minced

1 teaspoon dried marjoram 1 teaspoon mustard seeds 1/2 teaspoon celery seeds Yogurt Sauce:

2 tablespoons olive oil

2 tablespoons fresh lemon juice Sea salt, to taste

1/4 teaspoon red pepper flakes, crushed

1/2 cup full-fat yogurt 1 teaspoon dried dill weed

Directions

Spritz the sides and bottom of the cooking basket with 2 teaspoons of olive oil.

In a mixing dish, thoroughly combine the ground pork, beef, egg, salt, black pepper, paprika, garlic, marjoram, mustard seeds, and celery seeds.

Form the mixture into kebabs and transfer them to the greased cooking basket. Cook at 365 degrees F for 11 to 12 minutes, turning them over once or twice.

In the meantime, mix all the sauce Ingredients and place in the refrigerator until ready to serve. Serve the pork koftas with the yogurt sauce on the side. Enjoy!

Pork Loin with Mushroom Sauce

(Ready in about 30 minutes | Servings 4)

Per serving:

416 Calories; 13.9g Fat; 15.2g Carbs; 55.1g Protein; 4.4g Sugars

Ingredients

2 pounds top loin, boneless 1 tablespoon olive oil

1 teaspoon Celtic salt

1/4 teaspoon ground black pepper, or more to taste 2 shallots, sliced

2 garlic cloves, minced

1 cup mushrooms, chopped

2 tablespoons all-purpose flour 3/4 cup cream of mushroom soup 1 teaspoon chili powder Salt, to taste

Directions

Pat dry the pork and drizzle with olive oil. Season with Celtic salt and pepper. Cook in the preheated Air Fryer at 370 degrees F for 10 minutes.

Top with shallot slices and cook another 10 minutes.

Test the temperature of the meat; it should be around 150 degrees F. Reserve the pork and onion, keeping warm.

Add the cooking juices to a saucepan and preheat over medium-high heat. Cook the garlic and mushrooms until aromatic about 2 minutes.

Combine the flour with the mushroom soup. Add the flour mixture to the pan along with the chili powder and salt. Gradually stir into the pan.

Bring to a boil; immediately turn the heat to medium and cook for 2 to 3 minutes stirring frequently. Spoon the sauce over the reserved pork and onion. Enjoy!

Pork Sausage with Baby Potatoes

(Ready in about 35 minutes | Servings 3)

Per serving:

640 Calories; 47.5g Fat; 27.4g Carbs; 24.3g Protein; 1.1g Sugars

Ingredients

1 pound pork sausage, uncooked 1 pound baby potatoes

1/4 teaspoon paprika

1/2 teaspoon dried rosemary leaves, crushed Himalayan salt and black pepper, to taste

Direction

Put the sausage into the Air Fryer cooking basket.

Cook in the preheated Air Fryer at 380 degrees F for 15 minutes; reserve.

Season the baby potatoes with paprika, rosemary, salt and black pepper. Add the baby potatoes to the cooking basket.

Cook the potatoes at 400 degrees F for 15 minutes, shaking the basket once or twice. Serve warm sausages with baby potatoes and enjoy!

Pork Shoulder with Molasses Sauce

(Ready in about 25 minutes + marinating time | Servings 3)

Per serving:

353 Calories; 19.6g Fat; 13.5g Carbs; 29.2g Protein; 12.2g Sugars

Ingredients

2 tablespoons molasses 2 tablespoons soy sauce

2 tablespoons Shaoxing wine

2 garlic cloves, minced

1 teaspoon fresh ginger, minced

1 tablespoon cilantro stems and leaves, finely chopped 1 pound boneless pork shoulder

2 tablespoons sesame oil

Directions

In a large-sized ceramic dish, thoroughly combine the molasses, soy sauce, wine, garlic, ginger, and cilantro; add the pork shoulder and allow it to marinate for 2 hours in the refrigerator.

Then, grease the cooking basket with sesame oil. Place the pork shoulder in the cooking basket; reserve the marinade.

Cook in the preheated Air Fryer at 395 degrees F for 14 to 17 minutes, flipping and basting with the marinade halfway through. Let it rest for 5 to 6 minutes before slicing and serving.

While the pork is roasting, cook the marinade in a preheated skillet over medium heat; cook until it has thickened.

Brush the pork shoulder with the sauce and enjoy!

Rustic Pizza with Ground Pork

(Ready in about 30 minutes | Servings 4)

Per serving:

529 Calories; 9.6g Fat; 65.5g Carbs; 37.9g Protein; 0.9g Sugars

Ingredients

1 (10-count) can refrigerator biscuits 4 tablespoons tomato paste

1 tablespoon tomato ketchup

2 teaspoons brown mustard 1/2 cup ground pork

1/2 cup ground beef sausage

1 red onion, thinly sliced

1/2 cup mozzarella cheese, shredded

Directions

Spritz the sides and bottom of a baking pan with a nonstick cooking spray.

Press five biscuits into the pan. Brush the top of biscuit with 2 tablespoons of tomato paste.

Add 1/2 tablespoon of ketchup, 1 teaspoon of mustard, 1/4 cup of ground pork, 1/4 cup of beef sausage. Top with 1/2 of the red onion slices.

Bake in the preheated Air Fryer at 360 degrees F for 10 minutes. Top with 1/4 cup of mozzarella cheese and bake another 5 minutes.

Repeat the process with the second pizza. Slice the pizza into halves, serve and enjoy!

Sausage and Mushroom Chili

(Ready in about 35 minutes | Servings 4)

Per serving:

569 Calories; 35.3g Fat; 33.1g Carbs; 33.1g Protein; 10.4g Sugars

Ingredients

1 tablespoon olive oil 1 shallot, chopped

2 garlic cloves, smashed

10 ounces button mushrooms, sliced 1/2 pound pork sausages, chopped

2 cups tomato puree

2 tablespoons tomato ketchup 1 teaspoon yellow mustard

1 cup chicken broth

2 teaspoons ancho chili powder

Salt and ground black pepper, to taste

1 (16-ounce) can pinto beans, rinsed and drained 1/2 cup cream cheese

Directions

Start by preheating your Air Fryer to 360 degrees F. Heat the oil in a baking pan for a few minutes and cook the shallot until tender about 4 minutes.

Add the garlic and mushrooms; cook another 4 minutes or until tender and fragrant.

Next, stir in sausage and cook for a further 9 minutes. Add tomato puree, ketchup, mustard, and broth. Stir to combine and cook another 6 minutes.

Add spices and beans; cook an additional 7 minutes. Divide between individual bowls and top each bowl with cream cheese. Enjoy!

Smoked Sausage with Sauerkraut

(Ready in about 35 minutes | Servings 4)

Per serving:

478 Calories; 42.6g Fat; 6.1g Carbs; 17.2g Protein; 2.1g Sugars

Ingredients

4 pork sausages, smoked 2 tablespoons canola oil 2 garlic cloves, minced 1 pound sauerkraut

1 teaspoon cayenne pepper

1/2 teaspoon black peppercorns 2 bay leaves

Directions

Start by preheating your Air Fryer to 360 degrees F.

Prick holes into the sausages using a fork and transfer them to the cooking basket. Cook approximately 14 minutes, shaking the basket a couple of times. Set aside.

Now, heat the canola oil in a baking pan at 380 degrees F. Add the garlic and cook for 1 minute. Immediately stir in the sauerkraut, cayenne pepper, peppercorns, and bay leaves.

Let it cook for 15 minutes, stirring every 5 minutes. Serve in individual bowls with warm sausages on the side!

Smoky Mini Meatloaves with Cheese

(Ready in about 50 minutes | Servings 4)

Per serving:

585 Calories; 38.4g Fat; 22.2g Carbs; 38.5g Protein; 14.6g Sugars

Ingredients

1 pound ground pork 1/2 pound ground beef

1 package onion soup mix

1/2 cup seasoned bread crumbs

4 tablespoons Romano cheese, grated 2 eggs

1 carrot, grated

1 bell pepper, chopped

1 serrano pepper, minced 2 scallions, chopped

2 cloves garlic, finely chopped 2 tablespoons soy sauce sauce

Sea salt and black pepper, to your liking Glaze:

1/2 cup tomato paste

2 tablespoons ketchup

1 tablespoon brown mustard 1 teaspoon smoked paprika 1 tablespoon honey

Directions

In a large mixing bowl, thoroughly combine all Ingredients for the meatloaf. Mix with your hands until everything is well incorporated.

Then, shape the mixture into four mini loaves. Transfer them to the cooking basket previously generously greased with cooking oil.

Cook in the preheated Air Fryer at 385 degrees F approximately 43 minutes.

Mix all Ingredients for the glaze. Spread the glaze over mini meatloaves and cook for another 6 minutes. Bon appétit!

Spicy Bacon-Wrapped Tater Tots

(Ready in about 25 minutes | Servings 5)

Per serving:

297 Calories; 26.1g Fat; 9.3g Carbs; 7.1g Protein; 3.2g Sugars

Ingredients

10 thin slices of bacon 10 tater tots, frozen

1 teaspoon cayenne pepper

Sauce:

1/4 cup mayo

4 tablespoons ketchup 1 teaspoon rice vinegar 1 teaspoon chili powder

Directions

Lay the slices of bacon on your working surface. Place a tater tot on one end of each slice; sprinkle with cayenne pepper and roll them over.

Cook in the preheated Air Fryer at 390 degrees F for 15 to 16 minutes.

Whisk all Ingredients for the sauce in a mixing bowl and store in your refrigerator, covered, until ready to serve.

Serve Bacon-Wrapped Tater Tots with the sauce on the side. Enjoy!

Sticky Dijon Pork Chops

(Ready in about 20 minutes | Servings 4)

Per serving:

307 Calories; 14g Fat; 8.3g Carbs; 33.9g Protein; 7.1g Sugars

Ingredients

1/4 cup soy sauce

2 tablespoons brown sugar 1/4 cup rice vinegar

1 pound pork loin center rib chops, bone-in Celtic salt and ground black pepper, to taste 1 tablespoon Dijon mustard

Directions

Thoroughly combine the soy sauce, brown sugar, and vinegar; add the pork and let it marinate for 1 hour in the refrigerator.

Sprinkle the pork chops with salt and black pepper. Spread the mustard, all over the pork chops.

Cook in the preheated Air Fryer at 400 degrees F for 12 minutes. Serve warm with mashed potatoes if desired.

Tacos Al Pastor

(Ready in about 50 minutes | Servings 3)

Per serving:

356 Calories; 14.4g Fat; 19.6g Carbs; 36.3g Protein; 6.8g Sugars

Ingredients

Pork:

1 pound pork loin 1 tablespoon honey

Sea salt and ground black pepper, to taste 1/2 teaspoon cayenne pepper

1/2 teaspoon garlic powder

1/2 teaspoon thyme 1 teaspoon olive oil Tacos:

1 tablespoon annatto seeds 1 tablespoon olive oil

1/2 teaspoon coriander seeds

1 clove garlic, crushed

1 tablespoon apple cider vinegar

1 dried guajillo chili, deseeded and crushed 3 corn tortillas

Directions

Pat dry pork loin; toss the pork with the remaining Ingredients until well coated on all sides.

Cook in the preheated Air Fryer at 360 degrees F for 45 minutes, turning over halfway through the cooking time.

In the meantime, make the achiote paste by mixing the annatto seeds, olive oil, coriander seeds, garlic, apple cider vinegar and dried guajillo chili in your blender.

Slice the pork into bite-sized pieces. Spoon the pork and achiote onto warmed tortillas. Enjoy!

Tender Spare Ribs

(Ready in about 35 minutes + marinating time | Servings 4)

Per serving:

443 Calories; 35.2g Fat; 10g Carbs; 20.5g Protein; 3.1g Sugars

Ingredients

1 rack pork spareribs, fat trimmed and cut in half 2 tablespoons fajita seasoning

2 tablespoons smoked paprika

Sea salt and pepper, to taste

1 tablespoon prepared brown mustard 3 tablespoons Worcestershire sauce 1/2 cup beer

1 tablespoon peanut oil

Directions

Toss the spareribs with the fajita seasoning, paprika, salt, pepper, mustard, and Worcestershire sauce. Pour in the beer and let it marinate for 1 hour in your refrigerator.

Rub the sides and bottom of the cooking basket with peanut oil.

Cook the spareribs in the preheated Air Fryer at 365 degrees for 17 minutes. Turn the ribs over and cook an additional 14 to 15 minutes. Serve warm. Bon appétit!

Texas Pulled Pork

(Ready in about 1 hour | Servings 3)

Per serving:

415 Calories; 10.7g Fat; 39.3g Carbs; 37.9g Protein; 21.7g Sugars

Ingredients

1 pound pork shoulder roast 1 teaspoon butter, softened

1 teaspoon Italian seasoning mix

1/2 cup barbecue sauce 1/4 cup apple juice

1 teaspoon garlic paste

2 tablespoons soy sauce 2 hamburger buns, split

Directions

Brush the pork shoulder with butter and sprinkle with Italian seasoning mix on all sides.

Cook in the preheated Air Fryer at 360 degrees F for 1 hour, shaking the basket once or twice.

Meanwhile, warm the barbecue sauce, apple juice, garlic paste and soy sauce in a small saucepan.

Remove the pork shoulder from the basket and shred the meat with two forks. Spoon the sauce over the pork and stir to combine well.

Spoon the pork into the toasted buns and eat warm. Bon appétit!

The Best BBQ Ribs Ever

(Ready in about 40 minutes | Servings 2)

Per serving:

492 Calories; 33.5g Fat; 26.8g Carbs; 22.5g Protein; 19.7g Sugars

Ingredients

1/2 pound ribs

Sea salt and black pepper, to taste 1/2 teaspoon red chili flakes

1 tablespoon agave syrup 1/2 teaspoon garlic powder 1/2 cup tomato paste

1 teaspoon brown mustard

1 tablespoon balsamic vinegar

1 tablespoon Worcestershire sauce

Directions

Place the pork ribs, salt, black pepper and red pepper flakes in a Ziplock bag; shake until the ribs are coated on all sides.

Roast in the preheated Air Fryer at 350 degrees F for 35 minutes.

In a saucepan over medium heat, heat all sauce Ingredients, bringing to a boil. Turn the heat to a simmer until the sauce has reduced by half.

Spoon the sauce over the ribs and serve warm. Bon appétit!

Alphabetical index

CPSIA information can be obtained
at www.ICGtesting.com
Printed in the USA
LVHW020932260521
688445LV00004B/438

9 781802 329315